Copyright © 2016 Elke Duerr. All rights reserved.

ISBN-10: 0-9966606-0-7

ISBN-13: 978-0-9966606-0-0

WOLVES AND HUMANS
A NEW STORY OF COEXISTENCE

For the Wolf Nation

and

My Great-Grandmother Johanna

Acknowledgments

I cannot even attempt to thank everybody who was involved in the birthing of this book, but I will do my best.

First, my deepest gratitude goes to the wolves. My life has never been the same since I started on the journey of working with and for the wolves. They have taught me so much about patience, standing your ground, being social, kind and compassionate, and about the joy of living, no matter what is happening all around us.

Furthermore, to the many kind people whose caring hearts love all things and beings wild. You are eternally appreciated and loved and have carried me along the path of being a voice for the voiceless.

Last but not least, to all the human animals who lent their talent, love, and images to the book project so it would become even more beautiful: Hannah Schenck, Lara Anderson, Justine Vallieres, Ernest Stevens IV, Niklas and Norbert Duerr, MarjaRia, Daniel Clay, LUSH. Tom Peek for North American wolf photos and the author's photo, Miha Krofel for the European wolf and wild animal photos, my grandfather Ernst, Stephanie Stevens for photos and info on the Oneida Nation, and everybody else who has been instrumental in the making of this book. You know who you are. Photos of Mexican Gray Wolves and other photos by the author.

Information about our wolves was gleaned over the years from various sources like biologists, the internet, wolf conservationists, ranchers, experience in wolf country, etc.

May this book aid in the understanding of what a wolf is and what a wolf does. May we all thrive in the web of life!

Welcome back, wolves of the wild world!

Prologue

This book is inspired by and contains my own story, which started when I was a child growing up in Germany. I was out walking with my grandfather one day and he explained that one particular piece of forest was called "The wolf trap." My ears perked up and I got really excited. "Where are they?" I asked him. "Oh, this is where our ancestors killed the last wolf, so you and I would be safe." He answered me. Instead of feeling safe, I got sad and angry at my ancestors and all the other people who had killed all the wolves.

"What did they do that for, Grandpa?" I asked him. "Now I will never get to meet them. I will bring them back, Grandpa!" I was determined to have wolves back in Germany again, even though back then I did not know about all the other countries that had killed off their wolves or had attempted to do so. I had no idea of what a country was and all I knew was that I wanted the wolves back where I lived.

I later moved to the US from Germany, specifically to live where there are still wild animals and wilderness. In 2011, I produced a documentary film about our last endangered Mexican Gray Wolves, the lobos. Its title is *Stories of Wolves-The Lobo Returns*, and you can watch it here: **https://vimeo.com/70654722**

This book is part of my contribution to the return of the wolves.

Now we have wolves back in Germany, wolves who reintroduced themselves and are starting to thrive, even though there are still people who do not like that fact.

I have included a section about wolves in Germany at the end of the book.

Please stay true to yourself and make a stand for the animals and wild lands that you love so much. It does not matter if it is hummingbirds, wolves, bees, mountain lions, or prairie dogs. They need you to speak up for them and be their voice and we need them here on this planet with us.

Wolf photos in this book feature Mexican Gray Wolves, Wolves in Yellowstone National Park and European Wolves.

Chapter 1
The Return Of The Wolves

"Mom, dad! There is a wolf in the woods behind our house!" Ernest came bursting in the door, all excited and happy. "I love wolves! They are so beautiful!"

"No, that can't be. The last wolf around here got killed a long time ago," answered his father. "Calm down, son. It was a dog."

Right after dinner Ernest went back to where he had met the wolf. He was gone, but Ernest could still spot the large tracks in the mud.

The sheer joy that had gone up and down his body from having met a wild and free being was still fresh. He could feel a tingling at the top of his head and his heart was melting with joy. He had tasted wolf medicine.

His family did not share his adventure. "No way, Ernest. We do not have wolves here. Have not had them for a long time." His mom had said to him on his way out the door. "Nobody in the village who has seen a wolf in the wild is still alive. It has been that long."

"Maybe it was not true after all and it was a dog." He sighed. Somehow he just knew it had been a wolf. The way he had looked at Ernest with those big yellow eyes, curious and unafraid, not wanting to please him like a dog would. The wolf had looked like he was not afraid of anything or anybody.

How Ernest had felt, so alive and happy and like something very special had touched his soul, something wild. He had literally run home the whole way. He had been that excited and happy.

"It was a wolf and I know it in my heart." He was sure of it. He must know because he was a member of the wolf clan in his village. His people called themselves the True People. Since ancient times they had accepted the wolf as an equal, had celebrated the wolves' presence on this earth with song and dance.

Until the wolf hunters had killed them all off in the 1900s. Now, apparently, the wolves had returned to the True People. Ernest was not able to grasp what that really meant. His heart felt happy and free.

Ernest went back again a few days later. Something was urging him to return to that wild spot in the forest. His heart knew it: "The wolves are calling me!"

There they were, two of them this time. A male and a female wolf, playing with each other in the fresh snow.

"Mom, dad! There are two wolves in the forest now! It is true! I have seen them with my very own eyes!"

"Ernest, calm down. They are stray dogs. It's sad, but we do not have wolves around here any more. Now eat your kale so you can be strong and healthy. End of debate!"

This time, Ernest's friend Lucia was visiting. "Ernest," she whispered in his ear. "I believe you. Let's go out again after dinner and see them."

After they had eaten their kale they went back to the clearing in the magical forest together. The wolves were still there.

"They are beautiful" whispered Lucia. "I love wolves!" She was not afraid of them at all. Neither was her friend Ernest.

The two wolves stood perfectly still, just like the boy and girl. They were looking at each other and liked what they saw: Fearless, bright, and curious animals and humans who were very interested in the beings that stood before them and meant no harm.

Time stood still. Then the wolves turned around and were gone!

"Welcome back! I love you!" shouted Lucia into the stillness. "We need to protect them for sure. Get the whole village to like them. Let's go!"

Back at the house they told everybody:

"We saw two wolves. They are real! They belong here! They have come back to the True People and we are so lucky!"

Ernest's mom and dad sighed. "Now we have two crazy wolf people in the house. Do your homework and forget about it! What were you doing out there so close to dark anyway?"

Ernest and Lucia could not forget about it. They kept their meeting with the wolves alive in their hearts and did not tell any of the adults about it any more.

As soon as some of the snow on the ground had melted a little, they went back.

"Be quiet, Ernest. I saw something moving behind the trees."

They curiously peeked through the trees: Three wolves were sniffing the ground in the forest clearing. Golden light was streaming through the leaves. The world stood still.

"Look, this is the big male we saw last time. I do not recognize the other two." Ernest was excited. Blood was rushing through his body. His little heart kept beating strong and steady in his chest.

"Welcome back, wolves! We love you!" He said to them under his breath. He did not want to disturb them.

This time the children went straight to Ernest's grandma's house. Her name was Maria and she loved all animals, wild and tame.

"We saw three wolves today, Grandma Maria! We love them! They have come back to us!"

Grandma Maria smiled. Her mom, Ernest's great-grandma, had met and lived around wild wolves when she was a little girl and had told Maria about them. Ever since her childhood she had been wanting to meet them, but had never seen a wolf or heard of a wolf sighting around the village.

"Let's go and meet them!" Her eyes were shining that happy glow.

"She believes us!" Lucia jumped up and down. "She believes us, Ernest!"

The three of them walked into the forest. The place was waking up from the long winter by the warm love of spring.

"There they are!" Grandma got all excited. After all, she was Ernest's grandmother and shared that feeling of excitement with him. "They are gray wolves, for sure. They are here to stay this time." Everybody was happy to see the wolves. Six pairs of gleaming eyes met.

"The female you saw last time is nursing her newborn babies in her den right now. These three are bringing her food and they can't wait for the puppies to come out so they can meet the little ones. Meanwhile they are feeding the new mom in the den so she can concentrate on her young and does not have to go hunting. It is not unlike when the people in the village cooked for your moms after you were born. The villagers bring casseroles and salads to their new moms in the community, the wolves bring deer legs.

"It is the puppy time of the year! I would not be surprised if we saw some puppies next time. You know, wolves have between two and seven puppies in a litter. About half of them die in their first year. Wolves live in families, just like we do. When they come back, everything is much healthier than before. We call them the police of the forest because they keep the herds of deer and elk running and strong."

Ernest and Lucia stared at her. She knew a lot, that grandma!

Grandma looked like a little girl again. She was so happy! Then her face changed.

"Please always keep your distance from the wolves like today and never follow them. Allow them to be wild and free and do not stalk them. Let them come to you and visit you on their own terms if they want to."

Grandma's face was very serious all of a sudden. "People are doing all kinds of silly things because they do not know how to behave around wild animals. They often want to take a picture of a wild one at any cost. They want to know more than others about a certain animal by encroaching on them too closely.

Others want to be the first one to see a wolf, which makes them special in their eyes. The truth of the matter is that nobody is special in nature. Everybody is equally important and has their place in the larger whole of things.

Some do not respect the animals. They just do not know that animals are our brothers and sisters on our path on this earth. We True People consider ourselves to be just one animal, the human animal among all the other animals.

We give the animals the same rights as we give to ourselves. To inhabit this planet, thrive, and be happy. Each animal is their own nation: There is the Deer Nation, the Wolf Nation, the Skunk Nation, and so forth.

They are mothers and fathers and brothers and sisters just like we are. We humans have learned many valuable things from the Animal Nations. You know, we have learned how to hunt and raise a family from the wolves. They are very much like us. They are also different from us human animals. They are their own nation. Animals have a right to just be themselves and not have to serve us humans."

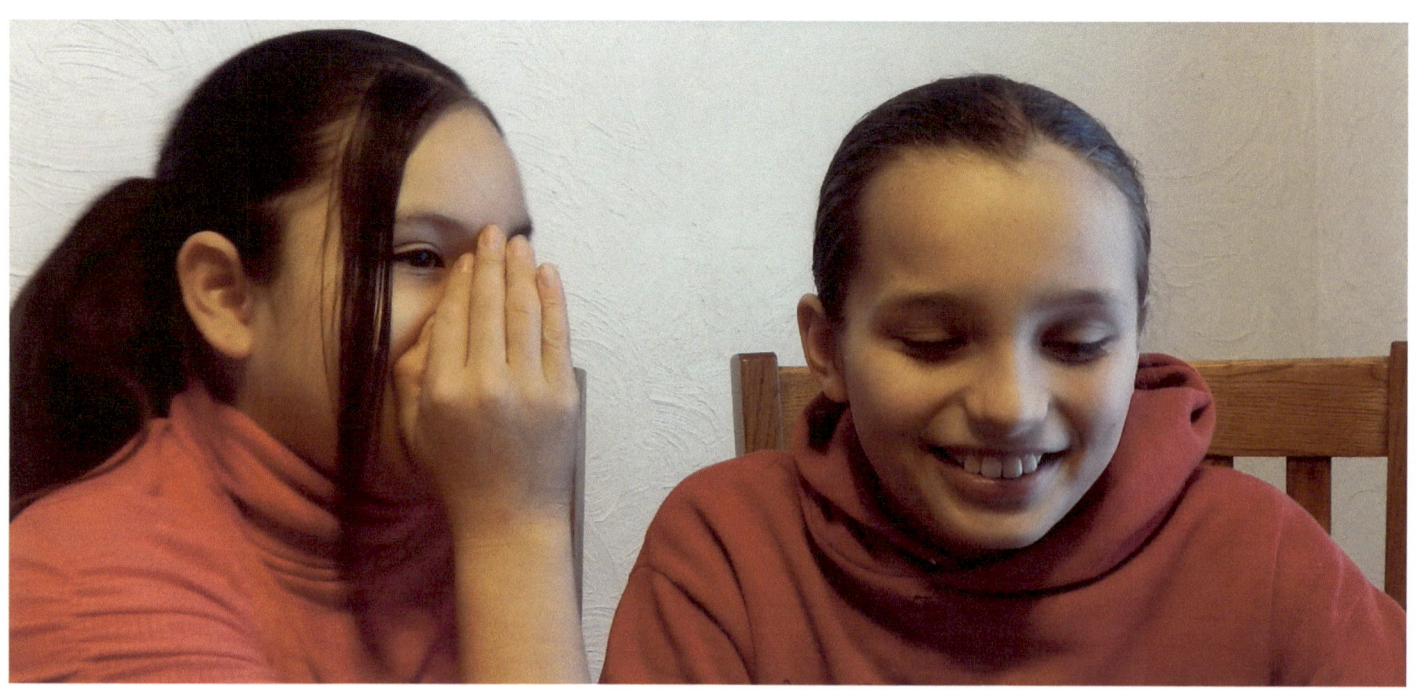

Lucia and Ernest nodded. They understood perfectly well what Grandma had just said to them. They just knew this to be true.

"We are the guardians of the rest of the ecosystem around here. It is our job to make sure that all the other life forms thrive. That includes the trees and plants as well. And the rocks."

"Why are people so afraid of wolves, Grandma?" Lucia was really worried about what would happen to the wolves when people found out about them.

"Much of it has to do with the old stories. We all know about a girl dressed in red or certain little pigs that have made the wolf the bad guy in the old stories. People made wild animals, especially the wolves, the bad guys because now we have domestic animals. Wolves sometimes kill a sheep or a cow. People were afraid to lose their livestock because of wolves.

That also meant losing their own lives because they had forgotten how to hunt or follow the herd of wild animals. Without domesticated animals, they were not able to survive any more. The truth is that we need everybody on this planet. Everybody was put on this planet for a reason.

That includes you and I", Grandma said and smiled at Ernest and Lucia.

"We will tell the people in the village about the wolves to make sure that everybody protects them and their sheep, cattle, and pets, and that they are not afraid of them. Let's make a plan when we get back to the house."

Chapter 2
The Web Of Life

Everybody in the village believed whatever Grandma said. They had much respect and love for her. She was wise and knew everybody. She would tell them all about the wolves, one by one. People had forgotten that there wasn't any danger coming from wolves. They did not attack and eat people like in the old fairy tales. People had lived without wolves for too long and did not know any more what it was like to have them around. Now they were sheepherders and cattle people. "During ancient times, long ago, we used to follow the herds of bison and elk and were nomads with summer and winter hunting grounds. Now we are stationary and do not move any more, and we protect what we own. In the olden days we did not have many possessions because we were moving all the time to follow the animals and were very much like the wolves. Free and on the move." Grandma Maria sighed. She took a deep breath and came back from her memories.

"I will call for a wolf blessing celebration. We have not had one in a long time. Since before the last wolves got killed. It is about time! How else will the wolves know that they are welcome and that we want them on this planet with us?

In the past, they were not welcome. The wildlife people and other hunters killed all the wolves in this area in favor of cattle and sheep. Back then people even thought that no wolves meant more elk and deer for the hunters. That is really silly. If wolves ate all the deer and elk they would starve and besides, there would not have been any large herds of deer and elk when the settlers came. Now we all know better! We get a second chance at being good guardians of our wolves." Grandma Maria was on fire.

"We have already lost some wolf species to extinction. There was one that followed the large herds of bison in the prairie. When the bison got almost killed off these wolves became extinct as well. Because the bison hunters realized that the bison were almost gone and that they now had to find other animals to kill for their fur. One was the wolf. Furthermore, the wolves no longer had their main food source when the bison were gone. That is how tied together everything is in this world. I will not allow that anything happens to these wolves. We will learn what it takes to keep them here on this planet with us. It is my new passion in life, to keep the wolves here in our community alive. I want to make sure that they thrive, that everybody thrives, really!"

At first people were a little afraid. They had heard so many old stories about wolves.

"Well, they did not eat me, nor Ernest or Lucia. So what is the big deal? Little Red Riding Hood is just a story that is not real. Besides, if we fear the wolves and show aggression towards them it will only cause unease and upset in the forest. We are True People and True People come from love for all the life forms on this planet. Do not let us forget that. Our ancestors used to be fearless and loving! They cared for their surroundings and environment, including all the animals."

"Wolves are shy creatures and are much more afraid of people than we are of them. They have every reason to be afraid of us. We have all but wiped them off the face of the earth."

"You will see, everybody will be safe." Grandma, Lucia, and Ernest did their best to make sure that people knew the truth about wolves.

Grandma was right. Nobody got eaten. Soon, the people lost their fear of wolves.

"What about our cows, sheep, dogs?" They worried. Worrying was what grown-up people did a lot in the village. They had forgotten the fearless and connected way of their ancestors and had adopted the way of worry.

"The wolves have not killed any animals from the village so far. They do not need to because they have plenty of deer and elk in the forest. That is what they prefer to eat anyway. They eat the old, sick, and weak deer and elk so that the herd stays strong and healthy."

The people nodded. That made sense!

"You just have to protect your cattle, goats, sheep, and pets better now that we have wolves around. Make sure your pets are on a leash and do not run after the wolves. The cows and sheep belong in a fenced in area and maybe we should get some Great Pyrenees sheep dogs. They really keep the wolves away. Our sheep bond with them and become their family members and the dogs protect them. The wolves usually respect the dogs' territory and stay away. It's as simple as that! We know better now, than to allow that they be killed off again. There are new ways to coexist with them that we are aware of nowadays. It is our responsibility to make an effort to coexist with all life forms on this planet.

Furthermore, our ancestors said that we naturally share the land, and our food, with all the other animals on this planet. It's not the end of the world if we lose some cattle to the wolves. What makes it acceptable for us humans to kill and eat a cow, but not for a wolf?"

Grandma Maria put her hands on her hips. "I will help you with the fencing and training of the dogs."

She told Ernest and Lucia one day when they were alone in the forest:

"Imagine now, how the story of the return of the wolves goes when we all know in our hearts that the earth, the wolves, the people, and the sheep and cows are one and the same life? Because we all come from the same life force, the same source of life. When we truly know that in our hearts again, what do you think will happen?"

"We will love and protect them all and will not think and act any more as if some animals are more important than others." Ernest chimed in right away.

"We see that we are just one part of the Whole, one little part, and that we humans are really caretakers of life. It is our job to make sure that everybody thrives" Lucia beamed. She loved those questions from Grandma. Grandma loved their answers.

"Yes, and sometimes the thriving of the herd of deer or elk means that the sick and weak ones become food for the wolves. What is that animal running in the distance?"

Just that moment, out of nowhere a bull elk appeared in the clearing in front of them, with four wolves in hot pursuit. In the blink of an eye, they were gone.

Grandma's eyes were still very sharp. They had taken in everything that happened.

"This elk has given himself to the wolves. He is old and sick. I can tell by his fur and by the way he is running. He will live on in the wolves. His death will be serving them just as much as the wolves are of service to the elk by keeping them healthy and running."

Grandma looked pensive. "You know, death is really nothing to be afraid of. Death is just a continuation of life, nothing more and nothing less. Our people have always known that. We have always lived very close to nature for many generations and have learned about her natural rhythms from her. Only in our more recent past have we started to forget. The wolves are helping us remember by returning to us."

Every time she walked through the village, Grandma Maria received many questions about the wolves. "What about our elk and deer? Will there still be any left for us humans to hunt? Are the wolves taking them all until there are none left for us?" A hunter was really afraid that his family might go hungry during the coming long winter. "I have not seen as many elk around the village this year." His brow was furrowed. He was worried.

"Our wolves will not eat all the deer and elk. Without food they would all starve. When there is not enough food around for them, they will not have puppies that year. No added hungry mouths to feed during a time of food shortage for them. That is how they are solving the food issue. The elk who were used to just standing around and browsing because there was no reason for them to move will now migrate around more. You will have to be a stronger hunter to kill a deer or an elk, that is all."

Again, Grandma Maria had the answer and the hunter left satisfied with it. He had taken on the challenge of being a stronger and more skilled hunter this season. He was already feeling good about it. There was much honor in being a strong hunter among the True People.

Slowly the villagers got used to the idea of having the wolves around. They could even hear them howl now and then. So far, only Ernest, Lucia, and Grandma Maria had actually seen them. The wolves were laying low as if they did not want to upset the villagers with their presence.

"They have the forest. We have the village and the fields and can coexist with them," Lucia's neighbor said.

"I kind of like how they howl. I am not afraid of them," Ernest's dad got excited after all. He believed what his mom, Grandma Maria said.

"They have given us our best friend, dog." A woman said, smiling. She was not afraid because wolves did not kill and eat people. They preferred deer and elk. She would take good care that her little lap dog stayed close to her and was on a leash during their walks in the woods.

"Absolutely no killing of wild animals just for fun, that includes wolves!" The village teacher taught her students early on. She went on to tell them more about this type of hunt. It was called the "Trophy Hunt."

"Some people are used to killing the biggest and strongest ones in a herd of deer or elk, and then mounting their antlers on a wall. Some hunters kill one of our last wild bison or Grizzly bears. What the hunters do not know is that the strongest animals need to multiply and pass on their genes. When only the smaller and weaker ones get to do that then the whole herd becomes weaker and the individual animals become smaller in size. Wolves and other animals that are carnivores take out the small and weak ones of all the animals in a herd. It would be way more difficult for them to hunt the big, healthy and fast ones. Hunting can be dangerous for the wolves. They might get kicked or otherwise injured."

This was a big one to digest. The students talked about it for days to come. It was about time that the True People knew about these things again!

Soon, it was clear. The wolves were welcome and they would hold a wolf blessing celebration for them. The people were even a little proud. Because it was so rare these days to have wolves around. They considered themselves lucky. In many places on this earth the wolves were gone forever and most likely would not return. What was even more exciting: their wolves chose to trust them and live near them in the forest. What an honor that was!

"When the animals do not run away from us in fear any more, then we can all coexist together. It will happen when we humans have taken our role as caretakers of this planet seriously." Grandma told them. "There has been a time when our ancestors lived in harmony with the other animals on the earth and knew their place in this world. A time when fear did not exist. Now we have been given the chance to live in a fearless and loving way again. We can choose to come from love for one another and not from anger and fear against each other."

Grandma glowed. She really had been waiting for this time to come and took her role in it very seriously. The return of the wolves! She knew what this meant for her people. They would be connected with the wildness inside of themselves again. Their newfound happiness was already more palpable. The return of the wolves was ringing in a new era of more closeness and connection to nature. The villagers were starting to remember what it meant to belong to the True People.

"I have hunted deer and my hunt was successful!" The doubtful hunter proudly told Grandma Maria one day. He brought her some meat from the animal that he had hunted to feed his family. His hunt was sacred. He knew to honor the animal he hunted and to share the meat. "The deer are much more alert now that the wolves are back. I talked to the spirit of the deer first and asked it to give its life to us freely."

Grandma Maria gladly accepted the gift from the hunter. "I know, you are a very skilled hunter. Thank you for thinking of the ancient custom of feeding the old, sick, and weak people first before you feed your family after you return from your hunt."

For a while, things were looking good for our wolves.

Until one day ...

Chapter 3
Wolves In Peril

"Ernest, wake up, wake up!" Lucia's face was all twisted up in a ball and tears were streaming down her face. "What is happening, what, what?" Ernest woke up from his deep sleep when his friend shook his arm. "The wolves have killed a sheep and now some of the villagers do not want them any more. Our wolves are in danger of being killed!" "No!" Ernest was fully awake and up and putting on his clothes in a second. "We must stop them! Let's go!" Mom shook her head in disbelief when she saw them running out the door. "How fast they can be when they care deeply about something", she thought.

The people were gathered in the village square. Angry voices were rising up into the air. "They are killing our sheep and cattle! We must stop them before there are hundreds of wolves around our village and there are no domestic animals left!" "This is just the beginning! Wolves are evil creatures! The stories about them are right!" "Let's keep calm and see what really happened." Grandma Maria's voice seemed small in all that chaos. Yet, everybody listened to her.

"Are you sure it was the wolves and not the coyotes or a mountain lion?" "Absolutely!" We saw their tracks all around the carcass of the poor dead sheep." "What difference does it make if a mountain lion, a wild dog, a coyote, a bear or a wolf takes down a sheep?" Grandma Maria tried to reason with the upset villagers. But to no avail! "Let's shoot the wolves!" "No! Let's call the wildlife people! They have traps and can trap them and move them somewhere else! Maybe to a zoo or wildlife park!"

When Ernest and Lucia heard those words, their hearts sank into their stomachs.

"That is worse than death! Life in a zoo for a wild animal, especially a wolf, is like being dead inside while their body is still alive. I have seen them in the zoo in the big city. They lose the fire in their eyes and walk around in circles all the time. We cannot do that to a wild animal. We cannot allow that!" Ernest was upset. Grandma Maria came over to where the horrified children were standing. "One dead sheep is not the end of the world. It's a blessing to share our food with the wolves. One dead sheep and the whole story of them versus us, of wolves versus sheep, has returned full force. Know that whatever is going on, I will not allow anything to happen to our wolves." Grandma Maria greeted Ernest and Lucia in the midst of all the chaos in the village. "Come on, my grandchildren! Let's do something! Quick!" Somebody in the crowd had a cellphone and was calling the wildlife people. "We do not have much time!" Ernest was determined.

All of a sudden, he saw the wild and intense face of the very first wolf he had ever come across in his life right before his eyes again. It spoke to him of innocence. "The wolves have not killed the sheep. I just know it! We have to find out who did it and fast! Who wants to come with me?" Ernest stood tall and very strong. Lucia and Grandma nodded. "Let's go!"

The crowd of angry people did not see them leave. The village was divided in half. Good wolf and bad wolf. The wildlife people were on their way with the wolf traps. Time was ticking away.

It did not take the three very long to find the sheep carcass. Ravens were flying above it and a coyote was close by.

"When a wolf kills a deer or elk, all the other animals benefit from it. The wolves eat first and then the coyotes, eagles, ravens, foxes, wolverines, bears, and other animals take their turns. The wolves are really helping the bears stay alive. When they come out of hibernation in the spring, they often eat on a wolf kill because it is the only food available to them then. Nature and her creatures are all one living system, one large web of life. Everybody is watching out for each other. When we take one animal out of this web of life, the whole web suffers."

"Some people think that an animal only has a right to live when they can 'use' it in some way. Eat its meat, wear its fur, drink its milk, or sell it in any way, shape, or form. For such people, wolves, of course, are useless and worthless animals. In their way of thinking wolves cause 'damage' to humans when they kill a 'valuable' cow or sheep. That justifies the killing of wolves in their eyes."

Again, Grandma was right. Her face was very pensive. "I will not allow that they take our wolves away. I did not wait for their return all of my life to see them killed or removed from their home now. We need the wild ones just as much as we need our domestic animals and pets. The mountains are lonely without them and the deer are getting slow and are multiplying way too fast and are starving because there are too many of them. They end up eating the geraniums in people's yards and hanging around their doors."

Yes, Ernest and Lucia could feel it. The whole ecosystem acted upset. The animals seemed to know that something was up and the usual calm had been replaced by an eerie stillness. Even raven, the trickster, the wordy and loud one, was quietly flying circles above the carcass.

Nobody else had touched it yet, but the animals that had killed it.

"When wolves kill a deer or elk, they run down the herd first to see who is limping or looks weak or skinny or has a disease. There seems to be an agreement going on between the hunter and the food. Like when we humans hunt an animal for food. The animal needs to agree to become our food before we kill her. Then she can give her power of life over to us when we eat her, and she will nourish us. Let's look at this sheep more closely."

Grandma walked over to the carcass and Lucia and Ernest followed her. "Let's not step on any of the tracks around it." They carefully inched closer without stepping on the tracks in the mud around the dead sheep. Ernest's heart sank. "They are definitely wolf tracks." Grandma Maria sighed. It was over!

Some part of her had hoped that it would not be so and that there would be a wolf friendly explanation to the dead sheep laying in the mud. Ernest took a long peek at them. Were they really? He looked at them more closely. They seemed a little smaller than the wolf tracks he had seen before in the snow and mud and sand. There were only two distinct sets of them that were the same size. His wolves always hunted in a family of four. Where were the puppy tracks? The puppies were now eating solid food and he had always seen their tracks around a dead deer or elk as well.

Something was fishy here. What was it?

He went into that deep, quiet space inside of himself. That place that just knows without being taught. Grandma called it his heart brain.

He was a picture of sheer concentration now. Nothing could distract him. He took in the view of the dead sheep, all sprawled out. It had bite marks all over its body. That was odd. "Grandma Maria, do wolves kill an animal like that? I have never seen that before when I came across one of their deer kills." "No, I do not think so." Grandma Maria was all activated.

Now she went inside to her heart brain. She needed to find out what really happened here. "Look!" Lucia pointed to a tuft of fur on one side of the sheep. It was brown. Not gray, black or white like the color of the wolves.

They stared at her hand that was holding the fur. It was curly. Wolf fur was never curly.

"This belongs to one of the wild dogs around here!" Grandma Maria was furious.

There were a couple of wild dogs around, a black one and a brown one. They had long been a thorn in her eyes for she knew that they were disturbing the peace of the forest by chasing after the wild animals. Sometimes the villagers were feeding them, but mostly they were fending for themselves. Now it looked like they had been killing a sheep.

"Can you see any black fur anywhere?" "Yes, here is a little tuft of it!" Lucia pointed to a black fur ball on the other side of the dead sheep.

"Wild dogs kill more sheep and cattle and are more dangerous to people than any other wild animal. They still have some of their instincts intact and start a chase. After they have killed an animal, they often do not know what to do with it. Hence they did not eat the sheep. We must stop that! Wild dogs are the culprits here and not the wolves."

They saw a car approaching and heading right towards them. It was the wildlife people. They wanted to have a look at the carcass before trapping the wolves. "The wolves did not do it! The wild dogs did it!" Ernest greeted them before they could say anything. "Let us have a look, son." The man came closer and started measuring the tracks, taking some fur and doing some tests.

"We will let you know in a few days what we found out." With that they drove off. Now it meant waiting for Ernest, Lucia, and Grandma.

It was a difficult few days for the three wolf people. The village was still split. Then came the news! It had been, indeed, a couple of dogs who took down the sheep.

The people went to fetch the dogs so that they would stop killing sheep. The dogs gladly went back to civilization with them. They really were domestic ones and did not have the skills any more to live in the wilderness. For them it was easier to be fed dog food and to be loved by humans.

Chapter 4
Coexistence Is Possible

The village breathed a sigh of relief!

"Let's have the celebration tomorrow!" Grandma Maria was determined again. She knew that after the return of the wolf celebration, the village would not be divided any more. It was to be a celebration for the wolves that included everybody. Grandma told Ernest and Lucia:

"It is likely that one of these days the wolves will kill one of the sheep or cows. That is just how it is. After all, we humans eat their food, the deer and elk. If we are strong and act as one people, if we help each other protect our livestock and watch out for them as if they were our family, there is a big chance it might never happen. You see, our cows and sheep once were wild as well. We domesticated them and now they are dependent on us. They often do not have their instincts intact enough any more to protect themselves. By domesticating them, we have taken on the job of protecting them. We are the ones who need to do it for them now. Sheep often will not run away when one of them gets killed. They just stand around and watch without their survival instincts kicking in. It is very sad, because sometimes they do not even protect their young ones from danger."

Ernest and Lucia were all ears. They had never thought of it that way!

"Yes," Grandma said. "We do not think about these things any more, but we really should. Because we need to take good care of our domestic animals as well. They need us, just as much as we need them."

The feast celebration came fast and the villagers gathered in the village square.

"Look, there is an eagle!" Ernest pointed to the bird circling high above them.

Deer gathered at the village edge. Raven flew ahead excitedly to tell the wolves of the ceremony.

Some of the men were drumming and chanting. The rest of the village danced the ancient wolf dance. They had almost forgotten how it went. It had been that long since there had been wolves around the village.

"Welcome, wolves. We want you here. We need you to keep the deer and elk strong. You are as important as the cows and the sheep. You belong here. Everybody belongs in the web of life. No exceptions."

Grandma Maria's voice was clear and very strong.

"Welcome wolves! We welcome our wolves!" everybody chimed in. "Welcome! We love you and want you here!" Lucia and Ernest shouted happily.

A tiny howl answered them from the forest. Another one chimed in and then two more.

"Their puppies are learning how to howl!" Grandma Maria's voice rose above the village once again. "They are thanking us!"

It was still again. Then, all of a sudden the whole wolf family started to howl. OW-WWWW! They were teaching their puppies how to howl!

"Beautiful!" somebody whispered. "Unlike anything I have ever heard before!" "The forest and the village are happy to have the wolves back! The forest was lonely without them." Lucia grinned from ear to ear with joy.

The people received one more blessing in return for blessing the wolves. When everybody was ready to go home, Ernest looked towards the forest.

"The wolves are here!" he said.

The villagers turned toward his outstretched hand, just in time to see four grown wolves and four puppies disappear into the forest way in the distance.

"I love wolves!" Ernest's little face beamed.

"I love our Wolf Nation! Just as much as I love dogs. They belong here! Everybody belongs in the web of life."

The beginning

A Guide For Readers, Students, Teachers and Parents

Example of an endangered wolf:

The Mexican Gray Wolf
Canis lupus baileyi

North America's most endangered land mammal

Our Mexican Gray Wolves are in danger of becoming extinct. Again ...

There were only seven left in the wild in Arizona, New Mexico, and Mexico, and only one of them was female when people realized that they were almost gone ... Then president Nixon signed the Endangered Species Act into law in 1973 and the Mexican Gray Wolf became an endangered species. People captured the last seven wolves alive and put them behind fences where they were breeding them. Their goal was to increase their number in the safety of captivity. In 1998 the first wolves were released back into the wild.

Now, in 2016, we have about 100 animals in the wild and 300 in captivity. That makes the Mexican Gray Wolf the most endangered land mammal in all of North America.

A Mexican Gray Wolf weighs about as much as a German Shepherd, around 60 to 85 pounds. Lone wolves are the exception. Most wolves live in a family with the mother, father, and pups from this and last year. They hunt and eat together and spend much time together, just like we humans do. When you see a wolf in the wild who is alone, that wolf is either out scouting to see where the deer and elk are, or taking a little stroll by himself. Chances are also that he or she has left their family in search of a mate and territory.

It takes 63 days for a wolf puppy to grow in her mother's belly. Just as long as it takes for a dog puppy to grow. Wolf mothers give birth to two to seven puppies in April or May. They are born in a den that she digs at a safe spot under a rock ledge, in a large burrow, or under a tree. The puppies are very small (around one pound) when they are born and really need their mom.

She only leaves the den to eat and drink when they are first born. The rest of her family feeds her and brings her meat. She has to go and get a drink of water occasionally, though. After about three to four weeks, the pups come out of the den for the first time. Then everybody is very happy. Uncles and aunts and big brothers and sisters are around; the whole family is there and they all help raise the puppies and protect them. Even so, half of the puppies die during their first year.

Nature made it that way so that the strong and healthy ones survive. Life as a wolf is not easy. Wolves can get hurt during hunting, sometimes there is not enough to eat, and other times there are diseases or humans kill them. A wolf lives about seven to 10 years in the wild. That is all.

They like to live in the forests and grasslands in New Mexico, Mexico and Arizona where they are safe from humans and can hide from them. They are very smart and have learned that humans are their enemies and have tried to kill them all off. It is very rare that you see a wolf in the wild. They see us and hear and smell us way before we have a clue that they are there and usually they run away from us. Their sense of hearing and smell and their vision are much better than ours. They do not only see in black and white, but also have blue and red photo receptors in their eyes. They hear well up to a frequency of 25 khz.

Wolves are carnivores, which means that their food consists of meat. A female wolf will only have puppies when she has enough meat to eat. Otherwise there will not be any puppies that year. The puppies nurse until they are old enough to eat regurgitated meat from their parents' stomachs. The adult wolves predigest food in their stomachs and when they get back to the den the youngsters lick their mouths and out comes the food, predigested!

Puppies have to learn everything from scratch, just like we did when we were little. They have to learn how and when to howl, wag their tail, growl, bark, yip, play, and mark their territory with urine and scat. Marking their territory is important because wolf families need a large amount of space to hunt.

Wolves need to tell other wolves in search of a territory that theirs is taken and to stay away. That is also one of the reasons why they howl: They want other wolves to stay away. Of course, sometimes they seem to talk to each other and tell their families where they are and if there is food in the area. You probably can think of a few more reasons why wolves howl.

A Guide For Readers, Students, Teachers and Parents

Another animal that is closely linked to the wolf is raven. Raven seems to be able to tell the wolves where the deer and elk are since he has the advantage of being able to fly and see what is going on where. When the wolves kill an animal for food, then raven gets his share along with many other animals. Wolves share their food with others and often, coyote is next after they feed on a carcass, then fox, raven, eagle, bear...

There are other things to consider about wolves. The Native American tribes and First Nations of Canada and the US have stories about them that are different from ours. They talk about Brother Wolf and how he taught them how to hunt and raise a family, how wolf gave them their companion, the dog; how wolf keeps the herds of deer and elk strong and how our lives are tied to the wolf: "Watch our Brother, the wolf. Whatever happens to him, will happen to all of us." They did not hunt the wolf, because they did not have sheep or cattle, but followed the wolf who led them to the herds of bison and deer and elk. Some of the tribes shared much of their territory with the wolves.

The Oneida Nation in Wisconsin, like some other First Nations have a wolf clan:

The Oneida Nation of Wisconsin has three clans: Turtle, Bear, and Wolf. The clan animals are like an ancient ancestor. Members of the Wolf Clan are looked at as relatives. Each clan has different duties and responsibilities. The wolf clan represents Family. Wolves belong in packs and work together as a family unit. For example, when pups are born, all the wolves in a pack help take care of the pups. The Oneida people all work together to take care of each other, especially the young. They are the future and Oneida are always looking forward seven generations. Wolves know the importance of family but they also have the strength and knowledge to stand alone. Wolves are strong leaders and are also known as the Pathfinders. Creator has designed a life path for us all, and the Wolves remind us to stay on our intended path.

Here is Ernest, a member of the Wolf Clan of the Oneida Nation:

Information About All The Other Wolf Subspecies

Two Subspecies: The Gray & Red Wolves

Red Wolves:

The Red wolf is smaller than the Gray wolf. They only weigh 40-50 pounds and hence eat small animals such as rabbits, squirrels, muskrats, and small deer. Their traditional home range included the Southeastern United States. There are less than 50 left in the wild as of February 2016.

Gray Wolves:

Our Arctic Wolves in the North, our Northern Rockies Wolves, our Timber Wolves, and Mexican Gray Wolves are all considered Gray Wolves even though they differ a lot in size, color, and what they eat.

Examples of other wolf subspecies who inhabit other places on this earth are:

The Eurasian Wolf, Canis lupus lupus, is one of the bigger wolves. Please do some research on this wolf and you will be amazed!

The Tundra Wolf, Canis lupus albus, lives in parts of Europe and Asia. Did you know that there are wolves in Israel, Iraq, Oman, Yemen, Jordan, and Saudi Arabia? They are called Arabian Wolf, or Canis lupus arabs.

The Tibetan Wolf lives in Central Asia from Turkestan, Tien Shan throughout Tibet, Mongolia, Northern China, and a few other places. Please do some research on this wolf and find out how big he/she is.

Among the extinct wolves are the Newfoundland Wolf who has not inhabited this earth since 1911, and the Bernard's Wolf. You can find information about them in books and on the internet.

Among the extinct wolves in the US are the Texas Wolf, Canis lupus monstrabilis; the Florida Black Wolf, Canis lupus floridanus; and the Cascade Mountain Wolf, Canis lupus fuscus.

The most amazing thing, though is that the wild dogs of Australia, Thailand, India, Indonesia, New Guinea, and the Solomon Islands, the Dingo or Canis lupus dingo, are also considered a subspecies of the wolf. So are our domestic dogs, or Canis lupus familiaris. Our dogs come from wild wolves way back. People have done selective breeding with them. They have developed into hundreds of dog breeds of various sizes, colors, and abilities. Just think of the specialized hunting dogs, or the little Chihuahua.

All wolves had been extinct in the lower 48 states in the US. Then in the 1990s, they were being reintroduced to Yellowstone National Park around the same time that the Mexican Gray Wolves were introduced to New Mexico and Arizona. People caught Timber Wolves in Canada and brought them down to YNP.

They multiplied and were doing well, but the dangerous thing for them is that they do not know the park boundaries. Human boundaries do not mean anything to wolves. They are not welcome outside of the park because there is cattle and other domestic animals. Sometimes they get killed just outside the park boundaries by hunters who are waiting for them to cross. Also, wolves need to migrate away from their family and find a mate and territory for themselves, not unlike humans. There literally aren't any other wolves outside of the park to form a family with. Now the wolves need to walk even further away from the safety of their family bonds and home territory to start their own family. This makes them very vulnerable to getting killed by humans.

Wolf Stories

Here are a few stories of wolves who have gone through almost heroic efforts to find a mate. Some have a happy ending, others do not.

Slavc and Juliette

Slavc, a radio collared male wild wolf from Slovenia in Europe, left his family in the middle of winter in search of a mate and territory.

He crossed the Austrian Alps that were covered in six feet of snow and continued on to Cortina d'Ampesso in Italy. Not far, in Lessinia, he found his Juliette, the only other wolf in the area. People named her Juliette since she was living close to Verona, where Romeo and Juliette was written. It was too late in the season to have puppies, but they continued on and had a litter of pups one year later.

The following spring, Slavc's collar fell off like it was intended to after 53 weeks of wearing it. Now we have to rely on eyewitness accounts on where the family is and what they are doing. It is better that way since they need some privacy to raise their family and since Slavc has given us so much information already. For a video about his story go here: **https://vimeo.com/48245301**

Echo

Echo, a female Gray Wolf, had traveled to the Grand Canyon from the Northern Rockies in late 2014 and was seen and filmed by visitors. She traveled on to Utah, probably in search of a mate and territory since there are no other wolves in the Grand Canyon area. This is where she died, near Beaver, Utah. A local hunter said that he mistook her for a coyote and shot her. Echo was named by a 10-year old boy after conservation groups held a naming contest for her. He said he chose the name Echo "because she came back to the Grand Canyon like an Echo does."

Journey

Journey, also known as OR7, is a male Gray Wolf who had been fitted with a radio collar and was tracked in Oregon and California. He is the first confirmed wolf in western Oregon since 1947, and the first in California since 1924. After he left his family in northeastern Oregon in September 2011 to search for a mate and territory, he wandered more than 1,000 miles through Oregon and Northern California.

Journey returned to the Rogue River watershed in the southern Cascade Range east of Medford, Oregon with a mate. In early 2015, officials named the two adult wolves and their young ones the Rogue Pack, the first wolf family in western Oregon. There are twelve wolf families and a minimum of 110 wolves in Oregon as of December 2015. Seven wolves died in Oregon in 2015.

One wolf family has since been documented in California.

The Return Of Our German Wolves

This is my favorite part and brings us back to the beginning of the book. As you remember, as a child, I always wanted the wolves to return to my home country, Germany. Back then, there were no wolves left. There were markers in the forest that read something like "Last wolf killed in 1872", "Last wolf in the area killed in 1750" and so on. It was quite discouraging. Then, something amazing happened! I was already living in the United States to be close to wild animals and wilderness when the first wolves crossed back into Germany from Poland. This time they were allowed free passage and made it all the way into Germany. The people who were working for the equivalent of the German Forest Service kept quiet about their return and waited to see what would happen. They did not kill them or tell many people about them which would surely have caused their early demise. They simply waited ...

The time had come that I had always dreamed about as a girl. The wolves were returning to the place where they belonged! The first wolf came in 1996 and the first wolf family was formed by two wolf parents in 2000. Since then, lots has happened! By 2006, ten years later, there were three families that had at least 18 puppies altogether that year.

Now, in 2016 there are about 150 wolves in Germany who live in 26 families. There even is a marker in the forest now that says "Return of the wolves".

I finally got one of my deepest wishes fulfilled! The German wolves have made their comeback and even though things are not ideal for them (some people in Germany still believe in the 'big, bad wolf' and there have been incidents of wolves getting poached) the wolves, are expanding their territory and there has even been a wolf sighting not too far from where I grew up. Please keep your fingers crossed that one day there will be a wolf family that lives near my home town.

Which brings me to a very important point:

I have seen wolves in Alaska, Arizona, Germany, Montana, New Mexico and Wyoming. Never has there even been the slightest sense of danger in me when I have come in contact with a wolf. On the contrary, a deep sense of awe and wonder has been the prevailing feeling. I have felt deep gratitude for this gift of a wolf sighting, because there are not that many wolves left in the lower 48 states and in many places, people will never get to see a wolf in the wild. Wolves have something to fear from us, not the other way round.

Every time we met, the wolves have come to me. They are very curious creatures and look at a human with these wonderful, fearless, deep, yellow eyes. I would never intrude on them since I respect the animals as beings who are here on this earth with me and everybody else. I grant them the same rights as I would any other being: the right to privacy, to be undisturbed, free of stress and free to do what they need to do here on this planet. I never follow them, want anything from them and rather invite them to come see me if they feel so inclined. I know, this is a stance that is not too common, but I am meeting increasingly more people who feel the same way and who are dedicating their lives to the welfare of humans, animals and the earth.

Maybe this book inspires you to be one of them?

Wolves and Humans

- Do you have any idea why European settlers did not like the Wolf?
- Why was their relationship to the Wolf different from that of the Native People?
- What stories about wolves do you know?
- How are they different from the story "The people who love wolves"?
- What can we do now, in the 21st century, to coexist with wolves?
- Why would we want them to stay on this earth with us?
- What is their role in the ecosystem?
- How do they influence other species of animals?
- What other animal is a descendent of the wolves and lives with us humans?
- What would you do when you see a wolf?
- Are you afraid of wolves? If yes, why? If no, why not?
- Do you know anybody in your family who is afraid of wolves?
- Who has ever seen a wolf in the wild?
- What was it like to see a wolf in the wild?
- What is the difference between a human killing and eating a cow and a wolf doing the same? Is there a difference?
- What is your own standpoint on coexistence between wild animals, livestock and humans?
- What can your contribution to coexistence look like?

Something Fun To Do & Find Out

Wolves are a keystone species. Please look up that term and explain why!

Please look up the term "Trophic Cascades." What is it and how do wolves fit into that term?

Talk to one person about wolves today and tell them something about them that they did not know before.

Do some research on how to coexist with wolves in modern times.

Is there an animal where you live that is in danger of becoming extinct? If yes: Can you do anything about it?

How can humans change and evolve their relationship with wild animals for our mutual benefit and thriving?

Quiz

1. Mexican Gray Wolves are:
a) carnivores
b) omnivores
c) herbivores
d) none of the above

2. They weigh about:
a) 100 pounds
b) 200 pounds
c) 40 pounds
d) 75 pounds

3. They live in:
a) herds
b) flocks
c) families
d) pods

4. Mexican Gray Wolves live in:
a) the city
b) forests and grasslands
c) parks and zoos
d) none of the above

5. Wolves howl to:
a) communicate with each other
b) say hi to the moon
c) exercise their vocal cords
d) warn deer and elk

6. Wolves are important because they:
a) are pretty
b) keep the herds of deer and elk strong
c) can howl
d) eat grass

7. Mexican Wolves are:
a) gray
b) rust
c) black and buff
d) all of the above

8. How many Mexican Wolves are there currently in the wild:
a) 100
b) 300
c) 80
d) none

9. Mexican Wolves carry food home for their pups in their:
a) mouths
b) paws
c) stomachs
d) none of the above

10. Mexican wolves are the:
a) prettiest wolves
b) most endangered wolves
c) fastest wolves
d) best wolves

11. Mexican wolves:
a) eat deer
b) eat elk
c) eat rodents
d) all of the above

Key: 1a, 2d, 3c, 4b, 5a, 6b, 7d, 8a, 9c, 10b, 11d

Epilogue

Thank you, dear reader, for taking the time to read this book. I hope that you learned some new things about our wolves, were able to open your heart towards them and that you can see why we need them on this planet with us.

If you would like to learn more about them, please do some research. There is still much to learn about them.

To order copies of "Wolves and Humans" please go here:

www.elkeeduerr.com or scan here:

Furthermore, I founded a nonprofit organization, the Web of Life Foundation, W.O.L.F. Please go here for more info on who we are and what we do:

www.weboflifefoundation.net or scan here:

There are multiple videos about wolves and other wild ones that I have completed over the years; please find them here:

https://vimeo.com/weboflife/videos or scan here: